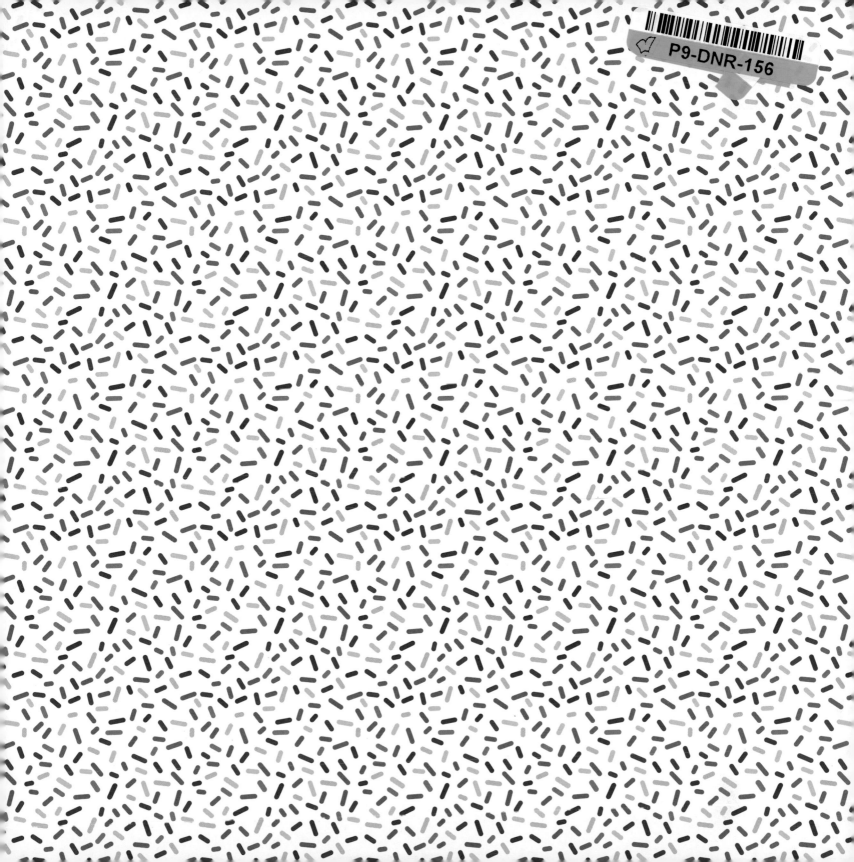

ICE CREAM Social!

Publications International, Ltd.

Microwave Cooking: Microwave ovens vary in wattage. Use the cooking times as guidelines and check for doneness before adding more time.

Let's get social!
@Publications_International
@PublicationsInternational
www.pilbooks.com

Contents

Fruit Fest

DOUBLE BERRY POPS

Makes 6 pops

2 cups plain nonfat Greek yogurt, divided

1 cup blueberries

3 tablespoons sugar, divided

6 (5-ounce) paper or plastic cups or pop molds

1 cup sliced strawberries

6 pop sticks

1 Combine 1 cup yogurt, blueberries and 1½ tablespoons sugar in blender or food processor; blend until smooth.

2 Pour mixture into cups. Freeze 2 hours.

3 Combine strawberries, remaining 1 cup yogurt and 1½ tablespoons sugar in blender or food processor; blend until smooth.

4 Pour mixture over blueberry layer in cups. Cover top of each cup with small piece of foil. Freeze 2 hours.

5 Insert sticks through center of foil. Freeze 4 hours or until firm.

6 To serve, remove foil and peel away paper cups or gently twist frozen pops out of plastic cups.

FRUIT FREEZIES

Makes 12 servings

1 **can (15 ounces) apricot halves in light syrup, rinsed and drained**

¾ **cup apricot nectar**

3 **tablespoons sugar, divided**

Ice cube trays

1 **can (15 ounces) sliced pears in light syrup, rinsed and drained**

¾ **cup pear nectar**

1½ **cups frozen chopped mango**

¾ **cup mango nectar**

Picks or mini pop sticks

1 Combine apricots, apricot nectar and 1 tablespoon sugar in blender or food processor; blend until smooth. Pour mixture evenly into one third of ice cube trays (8 cubes).

2 Combine pears, pear nectar and 1 tablespoon sugar in blender or food processor; blend until smooth. Pour mixture evenly into one third of ice cube trays (8 cubes).

3 Combine mango, mango nectar and remaining 1 tablespoon sugar in blender or food processor; blend until smooth. Pour mixture evenly into remaining one third of ice cube tray (8 cubes).

4 Freeze 1 to 2 hours or until almost firm.

5 Insert picks. Freeze 1 to 2 hours or until firm.

6 To remove pops from trays, place bottoms of ice cube trays under warm running water until loosened. Press firmly on bottoms to release. (Do not twist or pull picks.)

Variations: Try any of these favorite fruit combinations or create your own! Use crushed pineapple and pineapple juice or add more flavor to the combinations above. Add coconut extract to the apricot mixture or almond extract to the pear mixture.

BLACKBERRY LAYERED POPS

Makes 4 pops

1¼ cups plain nonfat Greek yogurt, divided

¼ cup milk

2 tablespoons sugar, divided

6 teaspoons lime juice, divided

1 cup chopped blackberries, divided

Pop molds or paper or plastic cups

Pop sticks

1. Combine ¾ cup yogurt, milk, 1 tablespoon sugar and 3 teaspoons lime juice in blender or food processor; blend until smooth. Gently stir in ¼ cup blackberries.

2. Pour mixture into molds. Freeze 1 hour.

3. Combine ½ cup blackberries and 1½ teaspoons lime juice in blender or food processor; blend until smooth.

4. Pour mixture into molds over yogurt layer. Freeze 1 hour.

5. Combine remaining ½ cup yogurt, ¼ cup blackberries, 1 tablespoon sugar and 1½ teaspoons lime juice in blender or food processor; blend until smooth.

6. Pour mixture into molds over blackberry layer. Cover top of each mold with small piece of foil. Insert sticks through center of foil. Freeze 4 hours or until firm.

7. To remove pops from molds, remove foil and place bottoms of pops under warm running water until loosened. Press firmly on bottoms to release. (Do not twist or pull sticks.)

LEMON STRAWBERRY POPS

Makes 4 pops

1 cup frozen strawberries

1 cup milk

½ cup plain yogurt

1 tablespoon sugar

1 tablespoon lemon juice

4 (5-ounce) paper or
   plastic cups or pop
   molds

4 pop sticks

1. Combine strawberries, milk, yogurt, sugar and lemon juice in blender or food processor; blend until smooth.

2. Pour mixture into cups. Cover top of each cup with small piece of foil. Freeze 2 hours.

3. Insert sticks through center of foil. Freeze 6 hours or until firm.

4. To serve, remove foil and peel away paper cups or gently twist frozen pops out of plastic cups.

WILD WATERMELON POPS

Makes 4 pops

2 **cups diced seedless watermelon (1-inch cubes)**

2 **tablespoons strawberry fruit spread**

1 **cup vanilla frozen yogurt**

4 **(5-ounce) paper or plastic cups or pop molds**

4 **teaspoons mini semisweet chocolate chips**

4 **pop sticks**

1 Combine 1 cup watermelon and fruit spread in blender or food processor; blend until smooth. Add remaining 1 cup watermelon; blend until smooth and well combined. Add frozen yogurt, ½ cup at a time, blending until smooth after each addition.

2 Pour mixture into cups. (See Tip.) Freeze 1 hour or until mixture just begins to harden.

3 Stir mixture in cups until smooth and slushy. Stir 1 teaspoon chocolate chips into each cup. Smooth top of mixture with back of spoon. Cover top of each cup with small piece of foil. Freeze 1 hour.

4 Insert sticks through center of foil. Freeze 4 hours or until firm.

5 To serve, remove foil and peel away paper cups or gently twist frozen pops out of plastic cups.

Tip: To use cone-shaped paper cups, line a baking sheet with regular-shaped 5-ounce paper cups, bottom sides up. Cut a small hole in the bottom of each regular-shaped paper cup. Place a cone-shaped cup, tip side down, in the hole to hold the pop in place.

FRUIT-FILLED POPS

Makes 4 pops

¼ **cup blueberries**

2 **strawberries, thinly sliced**

4 **kiwi slices**

Pop molds

⅔ **cup light-colored juice or flavored beverage**

Pop sticks

1 Evenly arrange blueberries, strawberries and kiwi in molds.*

2 Pour juice evenly into molds. Cover top of each mold with small piece of foil. Insert sticks through center of foil. Freeze 6 to 8 hours or until firm.

3 To remove pops from molds, remove foil and place bottoms of pops under warm running water until loosened. Press firmly on bottoms to release. (Do not twist or pull sticks.)

Plastic pop molds must be used for this recipe. The fruit will not stay in place if using paper or plastic cups.

Variation: This pretty pop works great with any combination of fruits. Choose any juice or flavored beverage that tastes best with the fruits.

MAGIC RAINBOW POPS

Makes about 6 pops

1 envelope (¼ ounce)
    unflavored gelatin

¼ cup cold water

½ cup boiling water

1 container (6 ounces)
    raspberry or
    strawberry yogurt

1 container (6 ounces)
    lemon or orange yogurt

1 can (8¼ ounces) apricots
    or peaches with juice

Pop molds with lids

1. Combine gelatin and cold water in 2-cup glass measuring cup. Let stand 5 minutes to soften. Add boiling water. Stir until gelatin is completely dissolved. Cool.

2. For first layer, combine raspberry yogurt and ¼ cup gelatin mixture in small bowl; stir until completely blended. Fill each pop mold about one third full with raspberry mixture.* Freeze 30 to 60 minutes or until set.

3. For second layer, combine lemon yogurt and ¼ cup gelatin mixture in small bowl; stir until completely blended. Pour lemon mixture over raspberry layer in each mold.* Freeze 30 to 60 minutes or until set.

4. For third layer, combine apricots with juice and remaining ¼ cup gelatin mixture in blender or food processor; blend until smooth. Pour mixture over lemon layer in each mold.* Cover with lids. Freeze 2 to 5 hours or until firm.**

5. To remove pops from molds, place bottoms of pops under warm running water until loosened. Press firmly on bottoms to release. (Do not twist or pull lids.)

*Pour any extra mixture into small paper cups. Freeze as directed in the tip.

**If you aren't using pop molds with lids, cover each pop with small piece of foil and insert sticks through center of foil.

Tip: Three-ounce paper or plastic cups can be used in place of the molds. Make the layers as directed or put a single flavor in each cup and cover each cup with small piece of foil and freeze 1 hour before inserting sticks. Freeze until firm. To serve, remove foil and peel away paper cups or gently twist frozen pops out of plastic cups.

APRICOT POPS

Makes 4 pops

1 can (about 8 ounces) apricot halves in heavy syrup

1 cup apricot nectar

½ cup plain nonfat Greek yogurt

Pop molds or paper or plastic cups

Pop sticks

1. Drain apricots; discard syrup. Rinse apricots under cool water; drain and chop.

2. Combine apricot nectar, yogurt and ¼ cup chopped apricots in blender or food processor; blend until smooth. Stir in remaining chopped apricots.

3. Pour mixture into molds. Cover top of each mold with small piece of foil. Freeze 1 hour.*

4. Insert sticks through center of foil. Freeze 4 hours or until firm.

5. To remove pops from molds, remove foil and place bottoms of pops under warm running water until loosened. Press firmly on bottoms to release. (Do not twist or pull sticks.)

*If using pop molds with lids, skip step 4 and freeze until firm.

PARADISE POPS

Makes 4 pops

1 cup milk

¾ cup frozen or fresh pineapple chunks

¾ cup frozen or fresh chopped mango

¼ cup unsweetened coconut milk

1 tablespoon honey

Pop molds or paper or plastic cups

Pop sticks

1 Combine milk, pineapple, mango, coconut milk and honey in blender or food processor; blend until smooth.

2 Pour mixture into molds. Cover top of each mold with small piece of foil. Freeze 1 hour.*

3 Insert sticks through center of foil. Freeze 6 hours or until firm.

4 To remove pops from molds, remove foil and place bottoms of pops under warm running water until loosened. Press firmly on bottoms to release. (Do not twist or pull sticks.)

If using pop molds with lids, skip step 3 and freeze until firm.

PURPILICIOUS POPS

Makes 4 pops

1 cup frozen blueberries

¾ cup pomegranate juice

½ cup raspberry sherbet

½ cup milk

2 tablespoons honey

Pop molds or paper or plastic cups

Pop sticks

1. Combine blueberries, pomegranate juice, sherbet, milk and honey in blender or food processor; blend until smooth.

2. Pour mixture into molds. Cover top of each mold with small piece of foil. Freeze 2 hours.*

3. Insert sticks through center of foil. Freeze 6 hours or until firm.

4. To remove pops from molds, remove foil and place bottoms of pops under warm running water until loosened. Press firmly on bottoms to release. (Do not twist or pull sticks.)

If using pop molds with lids, skip step 3 and freeze until firm.

TROPIC POPS

Makes 8 pops

Ingredients

- 2 bananas, broken into chunks
- 1½ cups unsweetened coconut milk
- 1½ cups pineapple juice
- 2 tablespoons sugar
- ½ teaspoon vanilla
- ⅛ teaspoon ground nutmeg
- ¼ cup flaked coconut
- 8 (5-ounce) plastic or paper cups or pop molds
- 8 pop sticks

Instructions

1. Combine bananas, coconut milk, pineapple juice, sugar, vanilla and nutmeg in blender or food processor; blend until smooth. Stir in flaked coconut.

2. Pour mixture into cups. Cover top of each cup with small piece of foil. Freeze 2 hours.

3. Insert sticks through center of foil. Freeze 6 hours or until firm.

4. To serve, remove foil and gently twist pops out of plastic cups or peel away paper cups.

Tip: Make these plain pops more appealing by using plastic cups, which give the pops a ridged texture.

CITRUS MANGO POPS

Makes 4 pops

1½ **cups mango nectar**

¾ **cup frozen chopped mango**

½ **cup lemon sorbet**

3 **tablespoons lime juice**

1 **tablespoon honey**

¼ **teaspoon grated lime peel**

Pop molds or paper or plastic cups

Pop sticks

1 Combine mango nectar, mango, sorbet, lime juice, honey and lime peel in blender or food processor; blend until smooth.

2 Pour mixture into molds. Cover top of each mold with small piece of foil. Freeze 2 hours.*

3 Insert sticks through center of foil. Freeze 6 hours or until firm.

4 To remove pops from molds, remove foil and place bottoms of pops under warm running water until loosened. Press firmly on bottoms to release. (Do not twist or pull sticks.)

If using pop molds with lids, skip step 3 and freeze until firm.

Chocolate Shoppe

TINY TOFFEE POPS

Makes 14 pops

1 pint (2 cups) chocolate ice cream

1½ cups chocolate-covered toffee chips

½ cup finely chopped blanched almonds

½ cup finely chopped milk chocolate

Pop sticks

1 Line small baking sheet with plastic wrap. Scoop 14 rounded tablespoonfuls ice cream onto prepared baking sheet. Freeze 2 hours or until firm.

2 Combine toffee chips, almonds and chocolate in shallow dish; mix well. Gently roll ice cream into balls in mixture, turning to coat and pressing mixture evenly into ice cream. Return to baking sheet.*

3 Insert sticks. Freeze 2 hours or until firm.

If ice cream melts on baking sheet, place baking sheet and ice cream in freezer 30 minutes before continuing. If ice cream is too hard, let stand 1 to 2 minutes before rolling in mixture.

WHITE CHOCOLATE MACADAMIA POPS

Makes 6 pops

¼ cup sugar

¼ cup cornstarch

½ teaspoon salt

2 cups milk

¾ cup whipping cream

6 ounces white chocolate, chopped

2 teaspoons vanilla

½ cup chopped macadamia nuts

6 (5-ounce) plastic or paper cups or pop molds

6 pop sticks

1 Combine sugar, cornstarch and salt in medium saucepan. Slowly whisk in milk and cream. Bring to a boil over medium heat, stirring constantly. Reduce heat to low; cook and stir 2 to 3 minutes or until thickened. Remove from heat.

2 Add white chocolate and vanilla, stirring constantly until chocolate is completely melted. Let stand 30 minutes to cool slightly.

3 Cover and refrigerate 2 hours.

4 Stir macadamia nuts into mixture. Pour mixture into cups. Cover top of each cup with small piece of foil. Freeze 2 hours.

5 Insert sticks through center of foil. Freeze 6 hours or until firm.

6 To serve, remove foil and gently twist frozen pops out of plastic cups or peel away paper cups.

CANDY ICE CREAM SUNDAE WITH HARD CHOCOLATE TOPPING

Makes 4 servings

- **1 pint vanilla ice cream, slightly softened**
- **½ to 1 cup chopped candy**
- **1 cup semisweet chocolate chips**
- **2 tablespoons coconut oil**

1. For ice cream, mix ice cream and candy in large bowl until combined. Cover bowl with plastic wrap; return to freezer to harden.

2. Meanwhile, prepare chocolate sauce. Combine chocolate chips and oil in medium microwavable bowl. Microwave on HIGH 30 seconds; stir. Microwave at additional 30-second intervals until melted and smooth.

3. Scoop ice cream into bowls. Pour chocolate sauce over ice cream. Allow to sit 30 seconds for sauce to harden.

FROZEN HOT CHOCOLATE POPS

Makes 6 pops

1 cup milk

2 ounces semisweet chocolate, finely chopped

3 tablespoons sugar

2 tablespoons hot chocolate mix

2 cups chocolate ice cream

Pop molds or paper or plastic cups

Pop sticks

1 Combine milk, chopped chocolate, sugar and hot chocolate mix in small microwavable bowl. Microwave on HIGH 30 seconds; stir. Microwave at 30-second intervals, stirring after each interval until chocolate is melted and mixture is smooth. Cool to room temperature, about 1 hour.

2 Pour chocolate mixture in blender or food processor; add ice cream. Blend until smooth.

3 Pour mixture into molds. Cover top of each mold with small piece of foil. Freeze 2 hours.*

4 Insert sticks through center of foil. Freeze 4 to 6 hours or until firm.

5 To remove pops from molds, remove foil and place bottoms of pops under warm running water until loosened. Press firmly on bottoms to release. (Do not twist or pull sticks.)

If using pop molds with lids, skip step 4 and freeze until firm.

CANDY BAR POPS

Makes 10 pops

1 pint (2 cups) vanilla ice cream

1 bar (about 2 ounces) chocolate-covered peanut, caramel and nougat candy, chopped

½ cup chopped honey-roasted peanuts

¼ cup caramel ice cream topping

Pop sticks

3 ounces semisweet chocolate

1. Scoop ice cream into chilled large metal bowl. Cut in chopped candy, peanuts and caramel topping with pastry blender or two knives; fold and cut again. Repeat until mixture is evenly incorporated, working quickly. Cover and freeze 1 hour.

2. Line small baking sheet with plastic wrap. Scoop 10 balls of ice cream mixture onto prepared baking sheet. Freeze 1 hour.

3. Reshape ice cream into balls, if necessary. Insert sticks; freeze 1 hour or until firm.

4. Melt chocolate in top of double boiler over simmering water, stirring occasionally. Drizzle melted chocolate over pops. Freeze 30 minutes to 1 hour or until firm.

CHOCOLATE-COVERED STRAWBERRY POPS

Makes 4 pops

1 **cup sliced strawberries, divided**

Pop molds

1 **cup chocolate ice cream**

¼ **cup milk**

3 **tablespoons chocolate syrup**

Pop sticks

1 Evenly arrange ½ cup strawberry slices in molds.*

2 Combine ice cream, remaining ½ cup strawberries, milk and chocolate syrup in blender or food processor; blend until smooth.

3 Pour mixture into molds. Cover top of each mold with small piece of foil. Insert sticks through center of foil. Freeze 6 to 8 hours or until firm.

4 To remove pops from molds, remove foil and place bottoms of pops under warm running water until loosened. Press firmly on bottoms to release. (Do not twist or pull sticks.)

Plastic pop molds must be used for this recipe. The fruit will not stay in place if using paper or plastic cups.

BROWNIE ICE CREAM TREATS

Makes 8 servings

½ **cup all-purpose flour**

½ **teaspoon salt**

¼ **teaspoon baking powder**

6 **tablespoons (¾ stick) butter**

1 **cup sugar**

½ **cup unsweetened Dutch process cocoa powder**

2 **eggs**

½ **teaspoon vanilla**

8 **(2¼-inch) jars with lids**

2 **cups pistachio or any flavor ice cream, slightly softened**

Hot fudge topping, heated (optional)

1. Preheat oven to 350°F. Spray 9-inch square baking pan with nonstick cooking spray. Combine flour, salt and baking powder in small bowl; stir to blend.

2. Melt butter in medium saucepan over low heat. Stir in sugar until blended. Stir in cocoa until well blended. Stir in eggs, one at a time, then vanilla. Stir in flour mixture until blended. Pour into prepared pan.

3. Bake 20 minutes or until toothpick inserted into center comes out with fudgy crumbs. Cool completely in pan on wire rack.

4. For 2¼-inch-wide jars, cut out 16 brownies using 2-inch round cookie or biscuit cutter. (See Tip.) Remove brownie scraps from pan (any pieces left between round cut-outs); crumble into small pieces. Save remaining brownies for another use.

5. Place one brownie in each of eight ½-cup glass jars. Top with 2 tablespoons ice cream, pressing to form flat layer over brownie. Repeat brownie and ice cream layers.

6. Drizzle with hot fudge topping, if desired, and sprinkle with brownie crumbs. Serve immediately or make ahead through step 5. Cover and freeze until ready to serve.

Tip: Measure the diameter of your jar first and cut out your brownies slightly smaller to fit in the jar. If your jar is not tall enough to fit two brownie layers, cut the brownies in half horizontally with a serrated knife.

COOKIES & CREAM POPS

Makes 3 pops

1 cup crushed mini creme-filled cookies (about 2½ cups cookies), divided

⅓ cup plus 1 tablespoon milk, divided

Pop molds or paper or plastic cups

1¼ cups vanilla ice cream

¼ cup mini semisweet chocolate chips

⅛ teaspoon ground cinnamon

Pop sticks

1. Combine ½ cup cookie crumbs and 1 tablespoon milk in small bowl, mixing and mashing with fork until blended. Press about 2 tablespoons crumb mixture into each mold, using wet fingers if necessary.

2. Combine remaining ½ cup cookie crumbs, ⅓ cup milk, ice cream, chocolate chips and cinnamon in blender or food processor; blend until smooth.

3. Pour mixture into molds over cookie base. Cover top of each mold with small piece of foil. Insert sticks through center of foil. Freeze 6 hours or until firm.

4. To remove pops from molds, remove foil and place bottoms of pops under warm running water until loosened. Press firmly on bottoms to release. (Do not twist or pull sticks.)

Chocolate Chip Cookie Pops: Scoop 1 pint (2 cups) vanilla ice cream into chilled large metal bowl. Cut in ⅔ cup chopped hard chocolate chip cookies and ⅔ cup chopped pecans with pastry blender or two knives; fold and cut again. Repeat, working quickly, until mixture is evenly incorporated. Scoop 10 scant ¼ cupfuls ice cream mixture. Gently roll ice cream into balls in 1 cup mini semisweet chocolate chips, turning to coat and pressing chips evenly into ice cream. Place on small baking sheet lined with plastic wrap. Insert sticks. Freeze 2 hours or until firm. Makes 10 pops.

ROCKY ROAD ICE CREAM

Makes about 1³/₄ quarts

⅔ cup Dutch process cocoa powder

¼ cup boiling water

1½ cups whole milk

1½ cups whipping cream

2 ounces unsweetened chocolate, finely chopped

6 egg yolks

1 cup sugar

1 teaspoon vanilla

1½ cups mini marshmallows

¾ cup toasted and coarsely chopped walnuts*

*To toast walnuts, spread in single layer on small baking sheet. Bake in preheated 350°F oven 8 to 10 minutes or until golden brown, stirring frequently.

1 Place cocoa in heavy medium saucepan; whisk in boiling water to make paste. Whisk in milk and cream. Bring to a simmer over medium heat, whisking often. Remove from heat.

2 Place chocolate in heatproof medium bowl and set wire sieve over bowl. Whisk yolks and sugar in another heatproof medium bowl about 1 minute or until pale and thickened. Gradually whisk in cocoa mixture. Pour into saucepan and cook over medium-low heat, stirring constantly with wooden spoon, until custard lightly coats spoon and instant-read thermometer reads 185°F. Immediately strain through sieve over chocolate. Let stand 3 minutes, then whisk until chocolate is melted and smooth. Stir in vanilla. Place bowl of custard in larger bowl of ice water. Let stand, stirring often, until chilled, about 1 hour.

3 Freeze mixture in ice cream maker according to manufacturer's directions until soft. Mix in marshmallows and nuts by hand.

4 Transfer ice cream to freezer containers. Freeze until firm, at least 2 hours. Scoop and serve.

FROZEN CHOCOLATE-COVERED BANANAS

Makes 4 servings

2 medium ripe bananas

4 pop sticks

½ cup granola cereal without raisins

1 bottle (7¼ ounces) quick-hardening chocolate shell dessert topping

1 Line small baking sheet with waxed paper.

2 Peel bananas; cut each in half crosswise. Insert stick about 1½ inches into center of cut end of each banana. Place on prepared baking sheet. Freeze 2 hours or until firm.

3 Place granola in large resealable food storage bag; crush slightly using rolling pin or meat mallet. Transfer granola to shallow dish. Pour chocolate shell topping in separate shallow dish.

4 Place one frozen banana in topping; turn and spread evenly over banana with spatula. Immediately place banana in dish with granola, turning to coat evenly. Return to baking sheet. Repeat with remaining bananas.

5 Freeze 2 hours or until firm. Let stand 5 minutes before serving.

Tip: For a fun twist on these treats, roll in sprinkles, coconut, chopped peanuts or any other desired toppings.

Cool Creations

FROZEN POLAR BEAR BITES

Makes 6 servings

1 **medium banana**

6 **pop sticks**

¼ **cup creamy peanut butter**

¼ **cup mini marshmallows**

2 **tablespoons unsalted dry-roasted peanuts, chopped**

1 **tablespoon chocolate sprinkles**

1 Cut banana into six equal pieces. Insert tips of sticks into peanut butter, then into banana pieces. Place on small waxed paper-lined baking sheet.

2 Combine marshmallows, peanuts and chocolate sprinkles in shallow dish.

3 Place peanut butter in small microwavable bowl. Microwave on HIGH 20 to 30 seconds or until melted and smooth.

4 Dip each banana piece in melted peanut butter, turning to coat evenly. Roll in marshmallow mixture. Place on prepared baking sheet; let stand until set.

5 Freeze 6 to 8 hours or until firm.

DREAMY ORANGE CREAMY POPS

Makes 8 pops

2 cups ice

1½ cups vanilla yogurt

¾ cup frozen orange juice concentrate

½ cup milk

¼ teaspoon vanilla

Pop molds with lids

1. Combine ice, yogurt, orange juice concentrate, milk and vanilla in blender or food processor; blend until smooth.

2. Pour mixture into molds. Cover with lids. Freeze 6 hours or until firm.*

3. To remove pops from molds, place bottoms of pops under warm running water until loosened. Press firmly on bottoms to release. (Do not twist or pull lids.)

*If using paper or plastic cups or molds without lids, cover each cup with small piece of foil. Freeze mixture 2 hours before inserting pop sticks through center of foil.

Tip: Frozen juice concentrate works great for frozen pops. Try any desired juice flavor and pair it with yogurt for a creamy fruity treat.

S'MORE POPS

Makes 6 pops

¼ cup plus 2 tablespoons fudge topping, divided

½ cup graham cracker crumbs

6 (3-ounce) paper or plastic cups or pop molds

1 cup marshmallow creme

¾ cup milk

1 cup vanilla ice cream

6 pop sticks

1 Place ¼ cup fudge topping in small microwavable bowl; microwave on HIGH 15 seconds. Stir until smooth.

2 Add graham cracker crumbs to melted fudge topping, mixing and mashing with fork until blended. Evenly divide mixture into cups; press mixture onto bottom of each cup, using wet fingers if necessary.

3 Combine marshmallow creme and remaining 2 tablespoons fudge topping in large microwavable bowl. Microwave on HIGH 20 to 30 seconds. Stir until smooth. Gradually whisk in milk.

4 Pour milk mixture in blender or food processor; add ice cream. Blend until smooth.

5 Pour mixture into cups over graham cracker base. Cover top of each cup with small piece of foil. Insert sticks through center of foil. Freeze 6 hours or until firm.

6 To serve, remove foil and peel away paper cups or gently twist frozen pops out of plastic cups.

BLACKBERRY SWIRL POPS

Makes 6 pops

1¼ **cups plain nonfat Greek yogurt**

¼ **cup milk**

2 **tablespoons sugar**

2 **tablespoons lime juice, divided**

1 **cup chopped blackberries**

Pop molds

Pop sticks

1 Combine yogurt, milk, sugar and 1 tablespoon lime juice in blender or food processor; blend until smooth.

2 Combine blackberries and remaining 1 tablespoon lime juice in blender or food processor; blend until smooth.

3 Alternately layer yogurt mixture and blackberry mixture in molds.* Using thin knife, create swirls by drawing knife up and down through layers.

4 Cover top of each mold with small piece of foil. Insert sticks through center of foil. Freeze 4 hours or until firm.

5 To remove pops from molds, remove foil and place bottoms of pops under warm running water until loosened. Press firmly on bottoms to release. (Do not twist or pull sticks.)

Plastic pop molds must be used for this recipe. The layers will not stay in place if using paper or plastic cups.

Tip: Another way to create thin swirls is by using a bamboo skewer or a thin round pop stick.

SALTED CARAMEL POPS

Makes 12 pops

1 pint (2 cups) vanilla ice cream

1 cup finely chopped salted pretzel sticks (about 2 cups whole pretzels)

¼ cup caramel ice cream topping

Coarse salt

Pop sticks

2 ounces semisweet chocolate

1. Scoop ice cream into chilled large metal bowl. Cut in pretzels and caramel topping with pastry blender or two knives; fold and cut again. Repeat, working quickly, until mixture is evenly incorporated. Cover and freeze 1 hour.

2. Line small baking sheet with plastic wrap. Scoop 12 balls of ice cream mixture onto prepared baking sheet. Freeze 1 hour.

3. Shape ice cream into balls, if necessary. Evenly sprinkle ice cream balls with salt. Insert sticks. Freeze 1 hour or until firm.

4. Melt chocolate in top of double boiler over simmering water, stirring occasionally.

5. Drizzle melted chocolate over pops. Freeze 30 minutes to 1 hour or until firm.

CHOCOLATE-HAZELNUT POPS

Makes 12 pops

1 cup raw hazelnuts

⅓ cup chocolate-hazelnut spread*

1 pint (2 cups) vanilla ice cream

Pop sticks

Can be found in most supermarkets near the peanut butter.

1. Spread hazelnuts in single layer in heavy-bottomed skillet. Cook over medium heat 2 minutes, stirring frequently, or until skins begin to peel and nuts are lightly browned. Transfer to clean dish towel. Rub hazelnuts to remove skins. Cool completely. Chop and set aside.

2. Line two small baking sheets with plastic wrap. Place plastic or acrylic cutting board in freezer 1 hour.

3. Meanwhile, drop 12 rounded teaspoonfuls chocolate-hazelnut spread onto one prepared baking sheet. Freeze 30 minutes or until firm.

4. Scoop ice cream onto frozen cutting board. Cut in chopped hazelnuts with pastry blender or two knives; fold and cut again. Repeat, working fast, until mixture is evenly incorporated.

5. Scoop 12 balls ice cream mixture onto second baking sheet. Place one frozen chocolate-hazelnut drop into center of each ball, gently pressing to enclose drop with ice cream.

6. Insert sticks. Freeze 2 hours or until firm.

RASPBERRY LAYERED POPS

Makes 4 pops

1¼ cups plain nonfat Greek yogurt, divided

¼ cup milk

2 tablespoons sugar, divided

6 teaspoons lemon juice, divided

1 cup chopped raspberries, divided

4 (5-ounce) paper or plastic cups or pop molds

4 pop sticks

1. Combine ¾ cup yogurt, milk, 1 tablespoon sugar and 3 teaspoons lemon juice in blender or food processor; blend until smooth. Gently stir in ¼ cup raspberries.

2. Pour mixture into cups. Freeze 1 hour.

3. Combine ½ cup raspberries and 1½ teaspoons lemon juice in blender or food processor; blend until smooth.

4. Pour mixture into cups over yogurt layer. Freeze 1 hour.

5. Combine remaining ½ cup yogurt, ¼ cup raspberries, 1 tablespoon sugar and 1½ teaspoons lemon juice in blender or food processor; blend until smooth.

6. Pour mixture into cups over raspberry layer. Cover top of each cup with small piece of foil. Insert sticks through center of foil. Freeze 4 hours or until firm.

7. To serve, remove foil and peel away paper cups or gently twist frozen pops out of plastic cups.

STRIPED PEANUT BUTTER & JELLY POPS

Makes 4 servings

4 teaspoons grape jelly

Pop molds

1½ cups vanilla ice cream

¼ cup milk

2 tablespoons creamy peanut butter

1 cup coarsely chopped peanut butter sandwich cookies (about 2½ cups cookies)

Pop sticks

1. Place jelly in small microwavable bowl. Microwave on HIGH 20 seconds or until melted. Cool until mixture has consistency of thick syrup.

2. Using tip of small spoon, drip 1 teaspoon melted jelly inside rim of each mold to form stripes. Place molds in freezer until needed.*

3. Combine ice cream, milk and peanut butter in blender or food processor; blend until smooth. Add cookies; blend until smooth.

4. Pour peanut butter mixture into molds. Cover top of each mold with small piece of foil. Insert sticks through center of foil. Freeze 6 to 8 hours or until firm.

5. To remove pops from molds, remove foil and place bottoms of pops under warm running water until loosened. Press firmly on bottoms to release. (Do not twist or pull sticks.)

Plastic pop molds must be used for this recipe. The jelly will not stick to paper or plastic cups.

ALMOND DELIGHT POPS

Makes 10 pops

4 ounces semisweet chocolate, divided

1 cup chopped plain macaroons (about 10 to 12 macaroons)

1½ cups sliced almonds, toasted*

1 pint (2 cups) vanilla frozen yogurt or ice cream

¼ cup strawberry jam

Pop sticks

*To toast almonds, spread in single layer in heavy-bottomed skillet. Cook over medium heat 1 to 2 minutes, stirring frequently, until lightly browned. Remove from skillet immediately. Cool before using.

1. Place plastic or acrylic cutting board in freezer 1 hour. Line small baking sheet with plastic wrap.

2. Meanwhile, melt 3 ounces chocolate in top of double boiler over simmering water, stirring occasionally. Remove from heat.

3. Gradually stir macaroon pieces into chocolate. Spread on prepared baking sheet. Freeze 30 minutes or until firm.

4. Spread almonds in shallow dish; set aside. Scoop frozen yogurt onto frozen cutting board. Cut in jam with pastry blender or two knives; fold and cut again. Gently mix in chocolate-covered macaroons.

5. Scoop 10 balls frozen yogurt mixture into almonds. Gently roll into balls, turning to coat and pressing almonds into frozen yogurt mixture. Place on prepared baking sheet. Freeze 1 hour.

6. Insert sticks. Freeze 1 to 2 hours or until firm.

7. Melt remaining 1 ounce chocolate in top of double boiler over simmering water, stirring occasionally.

8. Drizzle melted chocolate over pops. Freeze 30 minutes to 1 hour or until firm.

Party Time

PEACHY POPS

Makes 8 pops

1 package (16 ounces) frozen sliced peaches, softened, but not completely thawed

2 containers (6 ounces each) peach or vanilla yogurt

¼ cup honey

8 (5-ounce) paper or plastic cups or pop molds

8 pop sticks

Assorted decorating sugars or sprinkles

1 Combine peaches, yogurt and honey in blender or food processor; blend until smooth.

2 Pour mixture into cups. Cover top of each cup with small piece of foil. Freeze 2 hours.

3 Insert sticks through center of foil. Freeze 6 hours or until firm.

4 Remove foil and peel away paper cups or gently twist frozen pops out of plastic cups.

5 Spread sugars on small plate; roll pops in sugar. Serve immediately.

CANDY BAR ICE CREAM

Makes about 1¹/₂ quarts

2½ cups half-and-half

¾ cup sugar

1 cup whipping cream

2 teaspoons vanilla

1½ cups chopped (½ inch or smaller pieces) candy bars, such as chocolate-covered toffee or peanut butter cups

1 Bring 1 cup half-and-half and sugar to a simmer in medium saucepan over medium heat, stirring often to dissolve sugar. Pour into heatproof medium bowl set in larger bowl of iced water. Stir in remaining 1½ cups half-and-half, cream and vanilla.

2 Let stand until chilled, stirring often, adding more ice as needed, about 1 hour. (Cream mixture can be covered and refrigerated overnight.)

3 Freeze mixture in ice cream maker according to manufacturer's directions until soft. Mix in chopped candy bars.

4 Transfer ice cream to freezer containers. Freeze until firm, at least 2 hours. Scoop and serve. (This ice cream is best served within 24 hours of churning.)

LITTLE LEMON BASIL POPS

Makes 16 pops

1¼ **cups plain nonfat Greek yogurt**

¼ **cup milk**

Grated peel and juice of 1 lemon

2 **tablespoons sugar**

2 **tablespoons chopped fresh basil**

Ice cube trays

Pop sticks

1 Combine yogurt, milk, lemon peel, lemon juice, sugar and basil in blender or food processor; blend until smooth.

2 Pour mixture into ice cube trays. Freeze 2 hours.

3 Insert sticks. Freeze 4 to 6 hours or until firm.

4 To remove pops from trays, place bottoms of ice cube trays under warm running water until loosened. Press firmly on bottoms to release. (Do not twist or pull sticks.)

CHOCOLATE-COVERED CHEESECAKE POPS

Makes 24 pops

1 package (8 ounces) cream cheese, at room temperature

⅓ cup sugar

1 teaspoon vanilla

1 cup whipping cream, chilled

¼ cup mini semisweet chocolate chips

Pop sticks

1 pound semisweet chocolate, chopped

Colored sprinkles

1. Beat cream cheese, sugar and vanilla in large bowl with electric mixer at medium-high speed until well blended.

2. Beat cream in separate large bowl at high speed until stiff peaks form. Gradually beat in cream cheese mixture, scraping down side of bowl after each addition. Gradually beat in chocolate chips. Cover; refrigerate 2 hours or until firm.

3. Line small baking sheet with parchment paper. Gently roll cheesecake mixture into 24 balls. Place on prepared baking sheet. Freeze 1 hour.

4. Insert sticks. Freeze 2 hours or until firm.

5. Melt chocolate in top of double boiler over simmering water, stirring occasionally.

6. Remove cheesecake balls from freezer. Dip in chocolate, rotating to coat evenly. Let excess chocolate drip off. Top evenly with sprinkles.

7. Return cheesecake pops to baking sheet. Freeze 1 hour or until firm.

MINI MEXICAN COFFEE POPS

Makes about 32 pops

¼ **cup ground dark roast coffee**

2 **(3-inch) cinnamon sticks, broken into pieces**

2 **cups water**

1½ **teaspoons sugar**

⅓ **cup cinnamon half-and-half***

½ **teaspoon vanilla**

Ice cube trays

Picks or mini pop sticks

*You may use any flavor half-and-half or milk.

1. Place coffee and cinnamon sticks in filter basket of coffee maker. Add water to coffee maker and brew according to manufacturer's directions.

2. Remove coffee from heat. Stir in sugar until dissolved. Cool to room temperature, about 1 hour.

3. Add half-and-half and vanilla to cooled coffee. Pour mixture into ice cube trays. Freeze 2 hours.

4. Insert picks. Freeze 4 to 6 hours or until firm.

5. To remove pops from trays, place bottoms of ice cube trays under warm running water until loosened. Press firmly on bottoms to release. (Do not twist or pull picks.)

PEANUTTY POPS

Makes 10 pops

¾ **cup chopped chocolate-covered peanut butter cups**

¼ **cup crunchy peanut butter**

1 **pint (2 cups) vanilla ice cream**

2 **cups chopped honey-roasted peanuts**

Pop sticks

1 Freeze chocolate-covered peanut butter cups 20 to 30 minutes.*

2 Line small baking sheet with parchment paper. Spread peanut butter in thin layer on prepared baking sheet. Freeze 20 to 30 minutes. Peel paper away from peanut butter.

3 Scoop ice cream into chilled large metal bowl. Cut in peanut butter cups and peanut butter with pastry blender or two knives; fold and cut again. Repeat, working quickly, until mixture is evenly incorporated. Cover and freeze 1 hour.

4 Line small baking sheet with plastic wrap. Spread peanuts in shallow dish. Scoop 10 balls ice cream mixture into dish. Gently roll into balls, turning to coat and pressing peanuts evenly into ice cream mixture. Place on prepared baking sheet. Freeze 1 hour.

5 Shape ice cream into balls, if necessary. Insert sticks. Freeze 1 hour or until firm.

Freezing the peanut butter cups will make sure the chopped pieces remain as chunks and do not mix in with the ice cream.

CHOCOLATE CHIP SANDWICH COOKIES

Makes 16 sandwich cookies

¾ **cup plus ⅓ cup packed brown sugar**

½ **cup (1 stick) butter, softened**

1 **egg**

1 **teaspoon vanilla**

¾ **teaspoon baking soda**

½ **teaspoon salt**

1¾ **cups all-purpose flour**

1½ **cups semisweet chocolate chips**

1 **quart strawberry or peach ice cream, softened***

Assorted sprinkles (optional)

*You may use any flavor of ice cream.

1 Preheat oven to 350°F. Line cookie sheets with parchment paper.

2 Beat brown sugar and butter in large bowl with electric mixer at medium speed 5 minutes or until light and fluffy. Add egg and vanilla; beat until well blended. Beat in baking soda and salt. Slowly add flour, beating at low speed until blended. Stir in chocolate chips. Drop heaping tablespoonfuls of dough 2 inches apart onto prepared cookie sheets.

3 Bake about 10 minutes or until cookies are just beginning to brown around edges but are still very soft in center. (Cookies will look underbaked.) Cool on cookie sheets 5 minutes; remove to wire racks to cool completely.

4 Spread heaping tablespoonful of ice cream onto bottoms of half of cookies. Top with remaining cookies. Roll ice cream sides into sprinkles, if desired.

TRIPLE CHOCOLATE POPS

Makes 3 pops

1 cup chocolate ice cream

¼ cup milk

1 tablespoon chocolate syrup

½ cup crushed chocolate wafers

3 (5-ounce) plastic or paper cups or pop molds

3 pop sticks

6 tablespoons quick-hardening chocolate shell dessert topping

1 Combine ice cream, milk and chocolate syrup in blender or food processor; blend until smooth. Add crushed wafers; pulse using on/off action until just combined.

2 Pour mixture into cups, filling two-thirds full. Freeze 1 hour.

3 Insert sticks. Spoon 2 tablespoons chocolate shell topping into each cup over ice cream layer. *Do not cover with foil.* Freeze 4 to 6 hours or until firm.

4 To serve, gently twist frozen pops out of plastic cups or peel away paper cups.

MONSTER ICE CREAM SANDWICHES

Makes 6 servings

1 **package (16 ounces) refrigerated cookie dough**

Decorating icing, assorted colors

Assorted candies and chocolate chips

2 **cups ice cream***

*You may use any flavor of ice cream.

1. Bake 12 cookies according to package directions. Remove to wire rack; cool completely.

2. Decorate flat sides of six cookies using icing and candies to create faces of monsters.

3. Place remaining six cookies on serving plate. Top each cookie with ⅓ cup ice cream. Top with decorated cookies. Serve immediately.

CHOCOLATE-DRIZZLED GRAPE SKEWERS

Makes 6 servings

2 **cups seedless grapes (green, red or a combination of both)**

Bamboo skewers

¼ **cup semisweet chocolate chips**

¼ **cup white chocolate chips**

1 Wash grapes; remove stems. Dry completely with paper towel. Thread grapes on skewers. Place on waxed paper-lined baking sheet (see Tip).

2 Place semisweet chocolate chips in small microwavable bowl; microwave on HIGH 1 minute. Stir. Microwave at 30-second intervals, stirring after each interval until smooth. Drizzle over grapes.

3 Place white chocolate chips in separate small microwavable bowl; microwave on HIGH 1 minute. Stir. Microwave at 30-second intervals, stirring after each interval until smooth. Drizzle over grapes.

4 Freeze 2 hours before serving.

Variation: You can also freeze the grapes completely and drizzle them with chocolate just before serving.

Tip: Use a rimmed baking sheet for this recipe. Rest the bamboo skewers against the rims and rotate them on the baking sheet to drizzle evenly with chocolate.

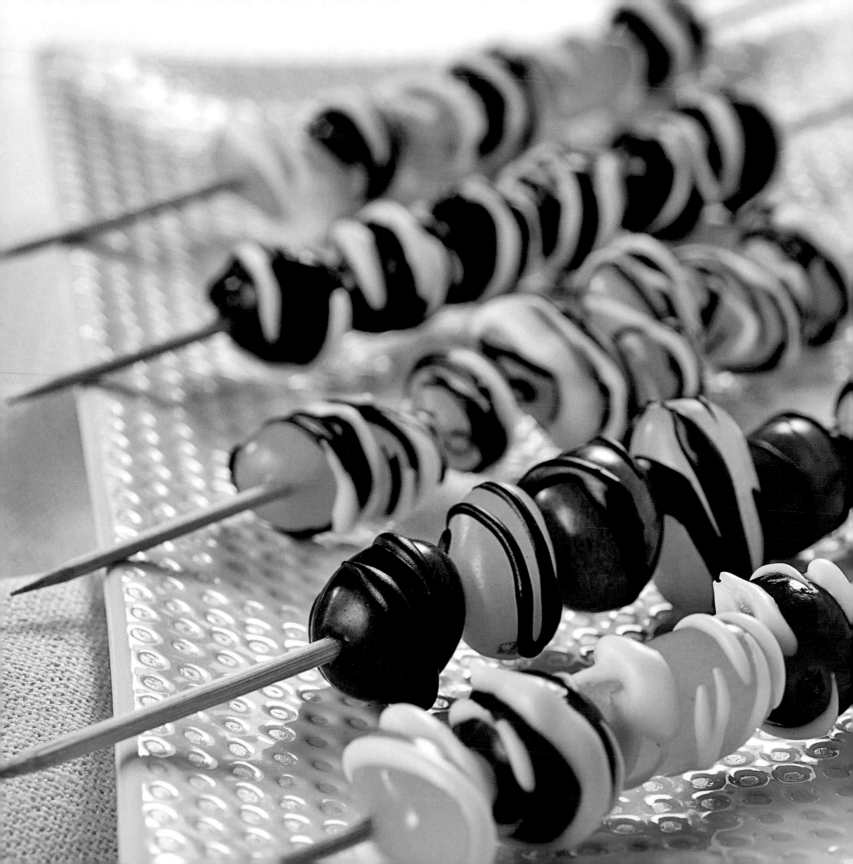

CHOCOLATE-COVERED ESPRESSO POPS

Makes 24 pops

1 container (about 9 ounces) chocolate sprinkles

1 pint (2 cups) chocolate ice cream or gelato

1 cup chocolate-covered espresso beans, coarsely chopped*

Pop sticks

*Chocolate-covered espresso beans are available in fine supermarkets and gourmet food stores.

1 Line medium baking sheet with plastic wrap. Spread chocolate sprinkles in shallow dish; set aside.

2 Scoop ice cream into chilled large metal bowl. Cut in chocolate-covered espresso beans with pastry blender or two knives; fold and cut again. Repeat, working fast, until mixture is evenly incorporated.

3 Scoop 24 rounded tablespoonfuls ice cream mixture into sprinkles. Gently roll into balls, turning to coat and pressing mixture evenly into ice cream. Place on prepared baking sheet. Freeze 1 hour.

4 Insert sticks. Freeze 1 hour or until firm.

Tip: Use coffee stirrers for the pop sticks to add a pop of color and make these frozen treats more fun!

Funky Flavors

CINNAMON-HONEY POPS

Makes 6 pops

1¼ **cups plain nonfat Greek yogurt**

½ **cup honey**

¼ **cup milk**

1 **tablespoon sugar**

½ **teaspoon ground cinnamon**

½ **teaspoon vanilla**

Pop molds or paper or plastic cups

Pop sticks

1. Combine yogurt, honey, milk, sugar, cinnamon and vanilla in blender or food processor; blend until smooth.

2. Pour mixture into molds. Cover top of each mold with small piece of foil. Freeze 2 hours.*

3. Insert sticks through center of foil. Freeze 4 hours or until firm.

4. To remove pops from molds, remove foil and place bottoms of pops under warm running water until loosened. Press firmly on bottoms to release. (Do not twist or pull sticks.)

If using pop molds with lids, skip step 3 and freeze until firm.

STRAWBERRY LEMONADE POPS

Makes 6 pops

½ **can (12-ounces) frozen lemonade concentrate, partly thawed**

1 **cup ice cubes**

½ **cup sliced strawberries**

½ **cup water**

6 **(3-ounce) paper or plastic cups or pop molds**

6 **pop sticks**

1 Combine lemonade concentrate, ice cubes, strawberries and water in blender or food processor; blend until smooth.

2 Pour mixture into cups. Cover top of each cup with small piece of foil. Freeze 1 hour.

3 Insert sticks through center of foil. Freeze 4 hours or until firm.

4 To serve, remove foil and peel away paper cups or gently twist frozen pops out of plastic cups.

Variation: If you love berries, make this pop even more flavorful and use raspberry lemonade concentrate.

Tip: These refreshing treats are perfect for a summertime barbecue.

FLUFFY PEANUT BUTTER POPS

Makes 4 pops

1 cup crushed peanut butter sandwich cookies (about 2½ cups cookies), divided

½ cup plus 1 tablespoon milk, divided

4 (5-ounce) paper or plastic cups or pop molds

¾ cup marshmallow creme

¼ cup creamy peanut butter

1¼ cups vanilla ice cream

4 pop sticks

1. Combine ½ cup cookie crumbs and 1 tablespoon milk in small bowl, mixing and mashing with fork until blended. Press 2 tablespoons crumb mixture into each cup, using wet fingers if necessary.

2. Combine marshmallow creme and peanut butter in large microwavable bowl. Microwave on HIGH 20 to 30 seconds. Stir until smooth. Gradually whisk in remaining ½ cup milk.

3. Pour milk mixture in blender or food processor; add remaining ½ cup cookie crumbs and ice cream. Blend until smooth.

4. Pour mixture into cups over cookie base. Cover top of each cup with small piece of foil. Insert sticks through center of foil. Freeze 6 hours or until firm.

5. To serve, remove foil and peel away paper cups or gently twist frozen pops out of plastic cups.

KEY LIME POPS

Makes 4 pops

1¼ cups vanilla ice cream

⅔ cup frozen limeade concentrate

¼ cup milk

Grated peel and juice of 1 lime

4 (5-ounce) paper or plastic cups or pop molds

4 pop sticks

1. Combine ice cream, limeade concentrate, milk, lime peel and lime juice in blender or food processor; blend until smooth.

2. Pour mixture into cups.* Cover top of each cup with small piece of foil. Freeze 2 hours.

3. Insert sticks through center of foil. Freeze 6 hours or until firm.

4. To serve, remove foil and peel away paper cups or gently twist frozen pops out of plastic cups.

   *To use cone-shaped paper cups, line a small baking sheet with regular-shaped 5-ounce paper cups, bottom sides up. Cut a small hole in the bottom of each regular-shaped paper cup. Place a cone-shaped cup, tip side down, in the hole to hold the pop in place.

CARROT CAKE POPS

Makes 8 pops

- 4 jars (4 ounces each) baby food carrots
- ½ cup milk
- 2 tablespoons granulated sugar
- 2 tablespoons packed light brown sugar
- 1 teaspoon ground cinnamon
- ½ teaspoon ground ginger
- ¼ teaspoon ground nutmeg
- ¼ teaspoon salt
- 2 cups vanilla frozen yogurt
  Pop molds
- ½ cup chopped glazed walnuts
  Pop sticks

1 Combine carrots, milk, sugars, cinnamon, ginger, nutmeg and salt in blender or food processor; blend until smooth. Add frozen yogurt; blend until smooth.

2 Pour mixture into molds. Freeze 1 hour.

3 Stir mixture in molds until smooth and slushy. Stir 1 tablespoon walnuts into each mold. Smooth top of mixture with back of spoon. Cover top of each mold with small piece of foil. Freeze 1 hour.*

4 Insert sticks through center of foil. Freeze 4 hours or until firm.

5 To remove pops from molds, remove foil and place bottoms of pops under warm running water until loosened. Press firmly on bottoms to release. (Do not twist or pull sticks.)

If using pop molds with lids, skip step 4 and freeze until firm.

ICE CREAM SANDWICHES

Makes 8 sandwiches

Candied Bacon (recipe follows), crumbled

1 package (18¼ ounces) chocolate cake mix with pudding in the mix

2 eggs

¼ cup warm water

3 tablespoons butter, melted

2 cups vanilla ice cream, softened

1. Prepare Candied Bacon.

2. Preheat oven to 350°F. Line 13×9-inch baking pan with foil; spray foil with nonstick cooking spray.

3. Beat cake mix, eggs, water and butter in large bowl with electric mixer until well blended. (Dough will be thick and sticky.) Press dough evenly into prepared pan; prick surface evenly with fork (about 40 times).

4. Bake 20 minutes or until toothpick inserted into center comes out clean. Cool in pan on wire rack.

5. Cut cookie in half crosswise; remove one half from pan. Spread ice cream evenly over cookie half remaining in pan.* Top with second half.

6. Freeze at least 4 hours. Cut into 8 equal pieces; dip sides in Candied Bacon. Wrap sandwiches and freeze until ready to serve.

If the ice cream is too hard to scoop easily, microwave on HIGH 10 seconds to soften.

Candied Bacon: Preheat oven to 400°F. Line 15×10-inch jelly-roll pan with heavy-duty foil. Coat both sides of 8 to 10 slices of bacon with ¼ to ½ cup packed brown sugar. Bake 18 to 20 minutes or until crispy. (Bacon should be turned over after 10 minutes).

CARAMEL CORN POPS

Makes 5 pops

½ cup frozen corn, thawed

½ cup milk, plus additional
   if necessary

1 cup half-and-half

2 tablespoons granulated
   sugar

2 tablespoons packed light
   brown sugar

1 egg yolk

⅛ teaspoon vanilla

½ cup chopped glazed
   pecans

5 (3-ounce) paper or
   plastic cups or pop
   molds

5 pop sticks

1. Combine corn and ½ cup milk in large saucepan. Partially cover and cook over very low heat 30 minutes. (If milk evaporates completely, stir in additional ¼ cup.)

2. Stir half-and-half and sugars into corn mixture. Cook, uncovered, over low heat until sugar is dissolved and liquid comes to a simmer, stirring frequently.

3. Beat egg yolk in small bowl. Whisk about ¼ cup corn mixture into egg yolk. Add mixture to saucepan; cook over medium heat 10 minutes or until slightly thickened, stirring constantly. Remove from heat. Stir in vanilla. Let stand 30 minutes to cool slightly.

4. Cover and refrigerate mixture 2 hours or up to 1 day.

5. Place mixture in blender or food processor; blend until smooth. Cover and refrigerate 2 hours or until slightly thickened.

6. Stir in pecans. Pour mixture into cups. Cover top of each cup with small piece of foil. Freeze 1 hour.

7. Insert sticks through center of foil. Freeze 6 hours or until firm.

8. To serve, remove foil and peel away paper cups or gently twist frozen pops out of plastic cups.

AVOCADO LIME ICE CREAM

Makes about 1½ quarts

4 **cups milk**

1 **cup sugar**

3 **egg yolks**

4 **ripe avocados**

Grated peel and juice of 2 limes

1 Combine milk and sugar in medium saucepan. Cook and stir over medium-high heat just until milk begins to boil; remove from heat.

2 Whisk egg yolks in medium bowl. Continue whisking while very slowly pouring in ¼ cup hot milk mixture. Slowly pour egg mixture into saucepan with remaining milk mixture. Cook over medium heat and whisk slowly until first bubble forms. *Do not boil.*

3 Pour mixture into medium bowl; cover and refrigerate 2 hours or until cold.

4 Cut avocados in half; remove pits. Scoop avocado pulp into mixture. Add lime peel and juice. Beat with electric mixer at medium speed until smooth; scrape bowl. Add chilled milk mixture; beat on low until blended.*

5 Freeze mixture in ice cream maker according to manufacturer's directions until soft.

6 Transfer ice cream to airtight containers and freeze several hours or until firm. Use within 1 week.

*For a smoother ice cream, strain mixture through a fine-mesh sieve.

CHEESECAKE BROWNIE POPS

Makes 8 pops

1 package (about 21 ounces) brownie mix, plus ingredients to prepare mix

8 (5-ounce) paper or plastic cups or pop molds

2 cups vanilla frozen yogurt

2 cups whipped cream cheese

1 cup half-and-half

¼ cup sugar

¼ teaspoon vanilla

8 pop sticks

1. Prepare brownie in 13×9-inch baking pan according to package directions. Cool completely in pan on wire rack.

2. Using bottom of paper or plastic cups, cut eight circles out of brownies. Place circles in bottom of each cup.

3. Combine frozen yogurt, cream cheese, half-and-half, sugar and vanilla in blender or food processor; blend until smooth.

4. Pour mixture into cups over brownie base. Cover top of each cup with small piece of foil. Freeze 2 hours.

5. Insert sticks through center of foil. Freeze 4 hours or until firm.

6. To serve, remove foil and peel away paper cups or gently twist frozen pops out of plastic cups.

Variation: If you want more brownies in this pop, stir ½ cup brownie chunks into the cheesecake mixture.

LITTLE LEMON-PISTACHIO POPS

Makes about 24 pops

1 **pint (2 cups) pistachio gelato**

⅓ **cup lemon curd**

2 **tablespoons chopped jalapeño-flavored pistachio nuts***

Grated peel of 1 lime

Ice cube trays

Pop sticks

You may substitute plain pistachio nuts.

1. Scoop gelato into chilled large metal bowl. Cut in lemon curd, pistachios and lime peel with pastry blender or two knives; fold and cut again. Repeat, working quickly, until mixture is evenly incorporated.

2. Evenly spoon mixture into ice cube trays. Freeze 30 minutes.

3. Insert sticks. Freeze 2 hours or until firm.

4. To remove pops from trays, place bottoms of ice cube trays under warm running water until loosened. Press firmly on bottoms to release. (Do not twist or pull sticks.)

Holiday Delights

MERRY MINT POPS

Makes 14 pops

1 pint (2 cups) peppermint
ice cream

½ cup crushed peppermint
candies (about
12 round candies)

½ cup chocolate sprinkles

Pop sticks

1 Line medium baking sheet with plastic wrap. Scoop 14 rounded tablespoonfuls ice cream onto prepared baking sheet. Freeze 2 hours or until firm.

2 Combine crushed peppermints and sprinkles in shallow dish. Gently roll ice cream into balls in mixture, turning to coat and pressing mixture evenly into ice cream. Return to baking sheet.*

3 Insert sticks. Freeze 2 hours or until firm.

If ice cream melts on baking sheet, place baking sheet and ice cream in freezer 30 minutes before continuing. If ice cream is too hard, let stand 1 to 2 minutes before rolling in mixture.

Tip: This recipe is best served the same day it is made. The candies will become soft and sticky over time.

GINGERY CHEESECAKE POPS

Makes 24 pops

1 package (8 ounces) cream cheese, at room temperature

⅓ cup plus 2 teaspoons sugar, divided

¼ cup minced crystallized ginger (optional)

1 teaspoon vanilla

1 cup whipping cream

¾ cup gingersnap cookie crumbs (about 15 to 18 cookies)

¼ cup ground pecans*

¼ teaspoon ground cinnamon

Pop sticks

To grind pecans, place in blender or food processor; blend until thoroughly ground with a dry, not pasty, texture.

1. Beat cream cheese, ⅓ cup sugar, crystallized ginger, if desired, and vanilla in large bowl with electric mixer at medium-high speed until well blended.

2. Beat cream in separate large bowl at high speed until stiff peaks form. Gradually beat in cream cheese mixture, scraping down side of bowl after each addition. Cover; refrigerate 2 hours or until firm.

3. Line large baking sheet with plastic wrap. Combine gingersnap crumbs, ground pecans, remaining 2 teaspoons sugar and cinnamon in shallow dish.

4. Scoop 24 rounded tablespoonfuls cheesecake mixture into gingersnap mixture. Gently roll into balls, turning to coat and pressing mixture evenly into cheesecake. Place on prepared baking sheet. Freeze 1 hour.

5. Insert sticks. Freeze 2 hours or until firm.

Serving Suggestion: For your holiday party, serve these pops in decorative miniature foil or paper baking cups. To make them even fancier, tie a ribbon around each stick.

BLEEDING POPS

Makes 6 servings

1 cup vanilla frozen yogurt

6 (5-ounce) paper or plastic cups or pop molds

1 cup raspberry sorbet

6 pop sticks

Red decorating gel

1. Place frozen yogurt in small microwavable bowl; microwave on LOW (30%) 10 seconds. Whisk and microwave at 10-second intervals until frozen yogurt reaches pourable consistency (about 5 times).

2. Evenly pour frozen yogurt into cups. Freeze 1 hour or just until set.

3. Place sorbet in small microwavable bowl; microwave on LOW (30%) 10 seconds. Whisk and microwave at 10-second intervals until sorbet reaches pourable consistency (about 5 times).

4. Evenly pour sorbet over frozen yogurt layer. Cover top of each cup with small piece of foil. Freeze 30 minutes.

5. Insert sticks through center of foil. Freeze 5 hours or until firm.

6. Remove foil and peel away paper cups or gently twist frozen pops out of plastic cups.

7. Pipe decorating gel down pops, allowing gel to drip down sides. Serve immediately.

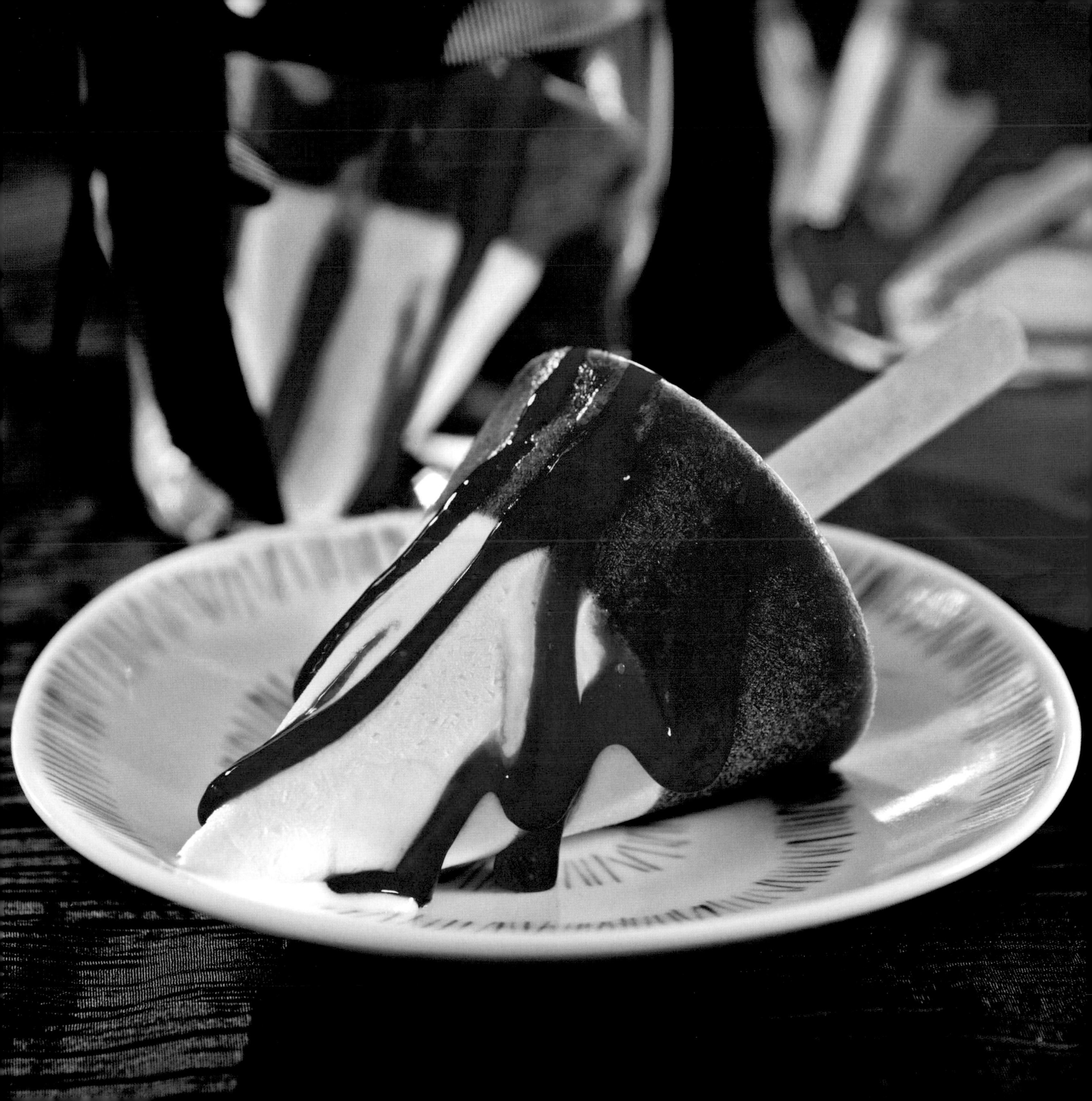

APPLE PIE POPS

Makes 4 pops

1 refrigerated pie crust
(½ of 15-ounce
package)

1½ teaspoons packed brown
sugar

1 tablespoon milk

4 (5-ounce) paper or
plastic cups or pop
molds

1¼ cups vanilla ice cream

1 cup apple pie filling

1 teaspoon pumpkin pie
spice

4 pop sticks

1. Preheat oven to 450°F. Line large baking sheet with parchment paper. Let pie crust stand at room temperature 15 minutes.

2. Roll pie crust onto prepared baking sheet. Prick with fork. Bake 10 to 12 minutes or until golden brown. Cool completely on baking sheet.

3. Crumble pie crust. Combine ½ cup crumbs and brown sugar in small bowl; mix well. Discard remaining crumbs or save for future use. Add milk to crumb mixture, mixing and mashing with fork until well blended. Press about 2 tablespoons crumb mixture into each cup, using wet fingers if necessary.

4. Combine ice cream, pie filling and pumpkin pie spice in blender or food processor; blend until smooth.

5. Pour ice cream mixture into cups over crumb base. Cover top of each cup with small piece of foil. Insert sticks through center of foil. Freeze 6 hours or until firm.

6. To serve, remove foil and peel away paper cups or gently twist frozen pops out of plastic cups.

PATRIOTIC POPS

Makes 4 servings

¾ **cup plain nonfat Greek yogurt**

2 **tablespoons lemon juice, divided**

1 **tablespoon milk**

1 **cup sliced strawberries**

½ **cup blueberries**

Pop molds

Pop sticks

1. Combine yogurt, 1 tablespoon lemon juice and milk in blender or food processor; blend until smooth.

2. Combine remaining 1 tablespoon lemon juice and strawberries in blender or food processor; blend until smooth.

3. Alternately layer blueberries, yogurt mixture and strawberry mixture in molds.* Cover top of each mold with small piece of foil. Insert sticks through center of foil. Freeze 4 hours or until firm.

4. To remove pops from molds, remove foil and place bottoms of pops under warm running water until loosened. Press firmly on bottoms to release. (Do not twist or pull sticks.)

*Plastic pop molds must be used for this recipe. The fruit will not stay in place if using paper or plastic cups.

Tip: Greek yogurt is yogurt from which much of the liquid or "whey" has been drained before use. It is available in most major grocery stores.

WINTER WONDERLAND POPS

Makes 10 pops

1 **pint (2 cups) vanilla ice cream**

½ **cup coarsely chopped macadamia nuts**

½ **cup chopped dried pineapple**

2 **tablespoons minced crystallized ginger**

2 **cups shredded sweetened coconut, toasted***

Pop sticks

*To toast coconut, spread in single layer in heavy skillet. Cook over medium heat 1 to 2 minutes until lightly browned, stirring frequently. Remove from skillet immediately. Cool before using.

1. Scoop ice cream into chilled large metal bowl. Cut in macadamia nuts, pineapple and ginger with pastry blender or two knives; fold and cut again. Repeat, working quickly, until mixture is evenly incorporated. Cover and freeze 1 hour.

2. Line small baking sheet with plastic wrap. Spread coconut in shallow dish. Scoop 10 scant ¼ cupfuls ice cream mixture into coconut. Gently roll ice cream into balls, turning to coat and pressing coconut evenly into ice cream. Place on prepared baking sheet. Freeze 1 hour.

3. Insert sticks. Freeze 1 hour or until firm.

Tip: Crystallized ginger can be found in the spice aisle of the grocery store.

ST. PATTY'S POPS

Makes 3 pops

½ cup crushed chocolate-covered mint cookies

⅓ cup plus 1 tablespoon milk, divided

3 (5-ounce) plastic or paper cups or pop molds

1¼ cups mint chocolate chip ice cream

3 pop sticks

6 tablespoons quick-hardening chocolate shell dessert topping

1. Combine cookie crumbs and 1 tablespoon milk in small bowl, mixing and mashing with fork until well blended. Press about 2 tablespoons crumb mixture into each cup, using wet fingers if necessary.

2. Combine remaining ⅓ cup milk and ice cream in blender or food processor; blend until smooth.

3. Pour mixture into cups over cookie base. Freeze 1 hour.

4. Insert sticks. Spoon 2 tablespoons chocolate shell topping into each cup over ice cream mixture. *Do not cover with foil.* Freeze 4 hours or until firm.

5. To serve, gently twist frozen pops out of plastic cups or peel away paper cups.

Tip: Make these plain pops more appealing by using plastic cups, which give the pops a ridged texture.

VALENTINE'S POPS

Makes 8 pops

4 ounces whipped cream cheese

2 cups cold milk, divided

1 package (4-serving size) white chocolate instant pudding and pie filling mix

½ cup thawed frozen raspberries, chopped

Pop molds or paper or plastic cups

Pop sticks

1. Stir cream cheese and ½ cup milk in large bowl until well blended. Add remaining 1½ cups milk and pudding mix; whisk 2 minutes. Cover; refrigerate 1 hour or until set.

2. Stir raspberries into mixture. Pour mixture into molds. Cover top of each mold with small piece of foil. Freeze 2 hours.*

3. Insert sticks through center of foil. Freeze 6 hours or until firm.

4. To remove pops from molds, remove foil and place bottoms of pops under warm running water until loosened. Press firmly on bottoms to release. (Do not twist or pull sticks.)

*If using pop molds with lids, skip step 3 and freeze until firm.

PUMPKIN PIE POPS

Makes 6 pops

½ **cup canned pumpkin pie mix**

½ **cup milk**

¼ **teaspoon vanilla**

1½ **cups vanilla ice cream**

6 **(5-ounce) paper or plastic cups or pop molds**

2 **containers (4 ounces each) prepared refrigerated vanilla pudding, divided**

3 **teaspoons packed brown sugar, divided**

6 **cinnamon sticks or pop sticks**

1. Combine pumpkin pie mix, milk and vanilla in blender or food processor; blend until smooth. Add ice cream; blend until smooth.

2. Pour 2 tablespoons mixture into each cup. Freeze 30 to 45 minutes or just until set. Cover; refrigerate remaining pumpkin mixture.

3. Combine 1 container vanilla pudding and 1½ teaspoons brown sugar; mix well. Spoon 1 tablespoon mixture over pumpkin mixture in each cup. Freeze 30 to 45 minutes or just until set.

4. Pour 2 tablespoons pumpkin mixture over pudding mixture in each cup. Freeze 30 to 45 minutes or until just set. Cover; refrigerate remaining pumpkin mixture.

5. Combine remaining 1 container pudding and 1½ teaspoons brown sugar; mix well. Spoon 1 tablespoon mixture over pumpkin mixture in each cup. Freeze 30 to 45 minutes or just until set.

6. Pour 1 tablespoon pumpkin mixture over pudding mixture in each cup. Cover top of each cup with small piece of foil. Freeze 30 to 45 minutes or just until set.

7. Gently insert cinnamon sticks through center of foil. Freeze 6 hours or until firm.

8 To serve, remove foil and peel away paper cups or gently twist frozen pops out of plastic cups.

Variation: To make this pop even more festive, add a layer of graham cracker crumbs or pie crust crumbs to either the top or bottom of the pop.

Metric Conversion Chart

VOLUME MEASUREMENTS (dry)

⅛ teaspoon = 0.5 mL
¼ teaspoon = 1 mL
½ teaspoon = 2 mL
¾ teaspoon = 4 mL
1 teaspoon = 5 mL
1 tablespoon = 15 mL
2 tablespoons = 30 mL
¼ cup = 60 mL
⅓ cup = 75 mL
½ cup = 125 mL
⅔ cup = 150 mL
¾ cup = 175 mL
1 cup = 250 mL
2 cups = 1 pint = 500 mL
3 cups = 750 mL
4 cups = 1 quart = 1 L

VOLUME MEASUREMENTS (fluid)

1 fluid ounce (2 tablespoons) = 30 mL
4 fluid ounces (½ cup) = 125 mL
8 fluid ounces (1 cup) = 250 mL
12 fluid ounces (1½ cups) = 375 mL
16 fluid ounces (2 cups) = 500 mL

WEIGHTS (mass)

½ ounce = 15 g
1 ounce = 30 g
3 ounces = 90 g
4 ounces = 120 g
8 ounces = 225 g
10 ounces = 285 g
12 ounces = 360 g
16 ounces = 1 pound = 450 g

DIMENSIONS

1/16 inch = 2 mm
⅛ inch = 3 mm
¼ inch = 6 mm
½ inch = 1.5 cm
¾ inch = 2 cm
1 inch = 2.5 cm

OVEN TEMPERATURES

250°F = 120°C
275°F = 140°C
300°F = 150°C
325°F = 160°C
350°F = 180°C
375°F = 190°C
400°F = 200°C
425°F = 220°C
450°F = 230°C

BAKING PAN SIZES

Utensil	Size in Inches/Quarts	Metric Volume	Size in Centimeters
Baking or	8×8×2	2 L	20×20×5
Cake Pan	9×9×2	2.5 L	23×23×5
(square or	12×8×2	3 L	30×20×5
rectangular)	13×9×2	3.5 L	33×23×5
Loaf Pan	8×4×3	1.5 L	20×10×7
	9×5×3	2 L	23×13×7
Round Layer	8×1½	1.2 L	20×4
Cake Pan	9×1½	1.5 L	23×4
Pie Plate	8×1¼	750 mL	20×3
	9×1¼	1 L	23×3
Baking Dish	1 quart	1 L	—
or Casserole	1½ quart	1.5 L	—
	2 quart	2 L	—